SPOTLIGHT ON OUR FUTURE

CLEAN WATER AND OUR FUTURE

KATHY FURGANG

NEW YORK

Published in 2022 by The Rosen Publishing Group, Inc.
29 East 21st Street, New York, NY 10010

Copyright © 2022 by The Rosen Publishing Group, Inc.

All rights reserved. No part of this book may be reproduced in any form without permission in writing from the publisher, except by a reviewer.

First Edition

Editor: Theresa Emminizer
Book Design: Michael Flynn

Photo Credits: Cover Damsea/Shutterstock.com; (series background) jessicahyde/Shutterstock.com; p. 5 Lukasz Pawel Szczepanski/Shutterstock.com; p. 6 Marco Ramerini/Shutterstock.com; p. 7 FOTOGRIN/Shutterstock.com; p. 8 Fouad A. Saad/Shutterstock.com; p. 9 Chris Overby/Shutterstock.com; p. 10 Smith Collection/Gado/Archive Photos/Getty Images; p. 11 Fratelli Alinari IDEA S.p.A./Corbis Historical/Getty Images; p. 12 Stephen J. Boitano/Getty Images; p. 13 Andrea Izzotti/Shutterstock.com; p. 15 Aaron P. Bernstein/Getty Images; p. 16 Riccardo Mayer/Shutterstock.com; p. 17 Martchan/Shutterstock.com; p. 18 paula french/Shutterstock.com; p. 19 Hindustan Times/Getty Images; p. 21 Rich Carey/Shutterstock.com; p. 22 Pcess609/Shutterstock.com; p. 23 MediaNews Group/Getty Images; p. 25 arindambanerjee/Shutterstock.com; p. 27 Richard Drew/AP Images; p. 29 Pantiwa Lakum/Shutterstock.com.

Cataloging-in-Publication Data

Names: Furgang, Kathy.
Title: Clean water and our future / Kathy Furgang.
Description: New York : PowerKids Press, 2022. | Series: Spotlight on our future | Includes glossary and index.
Identifiers: ISBN 9781725323742 (pbk.) | ISBN 9781725323773 (library bound) | ISBN 9781725323759 (6 pack)
Subjects: LCSH: Subjects: LCSH: Water-supply--Juvenile literature. | Water quality--Juvenile literature. | Water--Pollution--Juvenile literature. | Water conservation--Juvenile literature.
Classification: LCC TD348.F87 2022 | DDC 363.6'1--dc23

Manufactured in the United States of America

Some of the images in this book illustrate individuals who are models. The depictions do not imply actual situations or events.

CPSIA Compliance Information: Batch #CSPK22. For further information contact Rosen Publishing, New York, New York at 1-800-237-9932.

CONTENTS

A WORLD OF WATER 4

ANCIENT WATER KNOWLEDGE 6

MOVING WATER. 8

CLEAN WATER IDEAS 10

HOLD THE SALT 12

WATER POLLUTION 14

WATER SHORTAGES 16

SOLVING THE PROBLEM. 18

THE PLASTIC PROBLEM 20

OCEAN PLASTIC. 22

WATER RIGHTS 24

THE WATER WARRIOR 26

HOW TO SAVE WATER 28

BE A WATER WARRIOR. 30

GLOSSARY 31

INDEX 32

PRIMARY SOURCE LIST 32

WEBSITES. 32

CHAPTER ONE

A WORLD OF WATER

Water covers 71 percent of Earth's surface. Land only covers 29 percent. That's why Earth is sometimes called the Blue Planet!

The 7.6 billion people on Earth need clean drinking water. With so much water, it seems as though there should be enough for everyone. But much of Earth's water is salty and can't be used for drinking or watering crops. Also, many streams, rivers, lakes, and oceans on Earth are connected. If one water source is **contaminated**, it can spread the pollution elsewhere. Billions of people don't have access to, or a way to get, water at all. Some of these people live in places that suffer from droughts, or dry periods.

In order to survive, everyone needs clean water. By working together, we can make sure everyone gets it.

There's so much water on Earth that the planet looks mostly blue from outer space.

CHAPTER TWO

ANCIENT WATER KNOWLEDGE

Some ancient peoples understood that clean water was very important. For humans, animals, and plants to live well, water must be free of toxins and diseases, or illnesses. Long ago, when people started to build **permanent** settlements, they needed clean sources of water, so they dug wells. They knew that water could easily become dirty. To avoid this, wastewater was kept away from wells so drinking water wouldn't be contaminated.

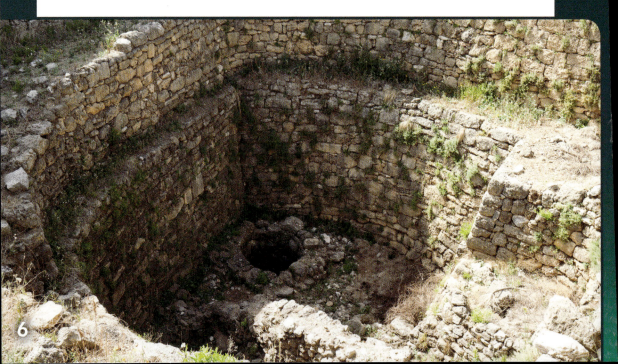

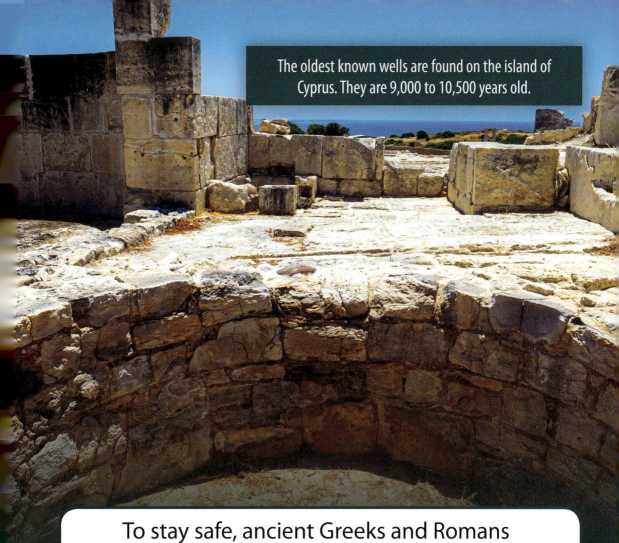

The oldest known wells are found on the island of Cyprus. They are 9,000 to 10,500 years old.

To stay safe, ancient Greeks and Romans knew to drink water that was clear and had no taste or smell. Many harmful things can easily enter water and pollute it. **Pesticides** and toxins can flow into Earth's waterways. **Microorganisms** from human and animal waste can contaminate growing vegetables. This is why people sometimes get sick from vegetables sold at the store.

7

CHAPTER THREE

MOVING WATER

Ancient cities were built around clean water sources. Most water on Earth is undrinkable salt water. The remaining 3.5 percent is fresh water. Almost 70 percent of Earth's fresh water is frozen in the polar ice caps. Finding, or making, drinkable fresh water is important.

Sometimes people need to find ways to move fresh water to communities. To move water to higher ground, the Egyptians used a water screw. This piece of **technology** is a pipe with a screw inside. When it's turned, it can move water from one height to another. Waste plants still use this tool so pipes don't get clogged.

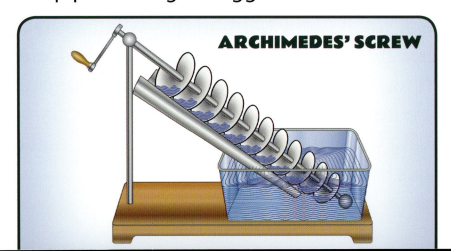

ARCHIMEDES' SCREW

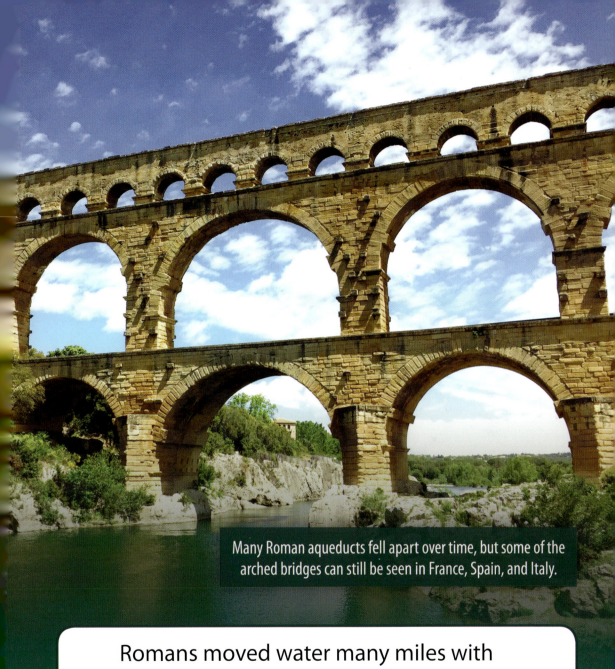

Many Roman aqueducts fell apart over time, but some of the arched bridges can still be seen in France, Spain, and Italy.

Romans moved water many miles with aqueducts. Aqueducts are systems that use pipes, canals, and bridges to carry fresh drinking water to cities that need it.

CHAPTER FOUR

CLEAN WATER IDEAS

Although ancient people created systems to move water, they didn't always know if the water was clean and safe to drink.

However, even in early times, people made efforts to clean their drinking water. Archaeologists, people who study human history through things left behind, have discovered that people knew ways to clean water as far back as 4000 BC. Ancient Sanskrit and Greek writings tell of ways of purifying, or cleaning, water, such as **filtering** it through **charcoal**, boiling it, exposing it to sunlight, and straining it.

WATER FILTRATION SYSTEM STILLWATER, MINNESOTA, 1912

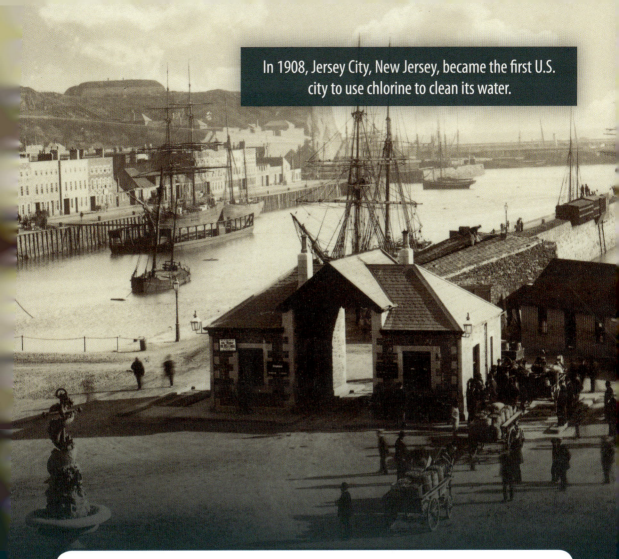

In 1908, Jersey City, New Jersey, became the first U.S. city to use chlorine to clean its water.

In the 1800s, scientists learned that microorganisms in the air and water sometimes spread diseases. This scientific breakthrough was called "germ theory." In 1804, Scottish engineer John Gibb invented a sand filter to clean water. Today, the chemical chlorine is used to kill germs we can't see.

CHAPTER FIVE
HOLD THE SALT

Scientists are working to invent better ways to clean water. A process called desalination takes salt out of ocean water, making it safe to drink. However, removing salt from water uses a lot of energy. It also costs about $2 to remove salt from 264 gallons (1,000 L) of ocean water. That's about how much water a person in the United States uses in two days. That's a lot more than fresh water costs.

PETER AGRE

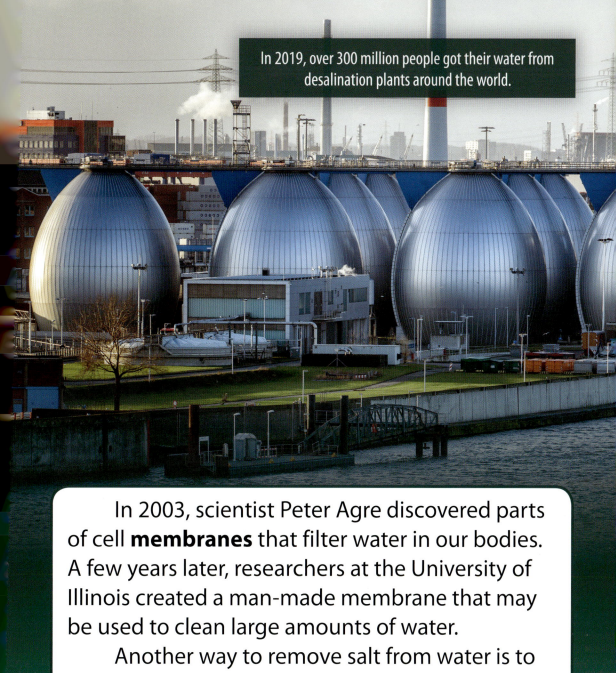

In 2019, over 300 million people got their water from desalination plants around the world.

In 2003, scientist Peter Agre discovered parts of cell **membranes** that filter water in our bodies. A few years later, researchers at the University of Illinois created a man-made membrane that may be used to clean large amounts of water.

Another way to remove salt from water is to boil the water and collect the clean steam. Still, people must find a way to safely store the leftover waste salt.

CHAPTER SIX
WATER POLLUTION

Sometimes accidents pollute water. In 2010, an oil drilling accident in the Gulf of Mexico spilled millions of gallons of oil into the ocean. Oil washed up on beaches in Louisiana, Mississippi, Alabama, and Florida. Millions of sea and land animals were killed.

In 2014, the city of Flint, Michigan, started getting water from the Flint River. People were told that the water was safe, but it smelled and tasted bad. Some people became sick. Doctors later found high levels of lead in children who were drinking the water. Lead is an element that can be very harmful. People learned then that the new water source was more **corrosive** than the old one. This caused lead from city pipes to seep into the drinking water, sickening thousands of people.

Amariyanna Copeny is a 12-year-old **activist**. She has spoken out about the ongoing water crisis in Flint, Michigan. Her nickname is "Little Miss Flint."

CHAPTER SEVEN

WATER SHORTAGES

Water isn't always easily available. Water shortage is also called water scarcity. This often happens in places where there are long droughts, there's no technology to clean water, or the available water isn't easy to get to.

Many people living in Africa have a hard time getting clean water. Droughts, bad supply systems, contamination, and conflicts contribute to this problem. Clean water sources have even been the cause of war in some parts of the world.

Water scarcity is a big problem in Africa.

 In many communities, women are responsible for getting clean water for their family. This means walking miles each day just to collect water. Altogether, women and girls spend about 200 million hours each day working to find water. Because of this, many girls don't have time to go to school.

CHAPTER EIGHT

SOLVING THE PROBLEM

Water scarcity can be a deadly issue. It can contribute to the spread of diseases, cause animals and people to suffer, and lead to **famine**.

Sometimes people have no choice but to drink unclean water or eat food contaminated by it. This can cause serious illnesses. Some of them cause dehydration, which is a dangerous shortage of water in the body. Around the world, 4 percent of deaths are caused by this kind of dehydration.

In places with bad droughts, animals have no drinking water either. In 2019, at least 200 elephants died in Zimbabwe because of drought.

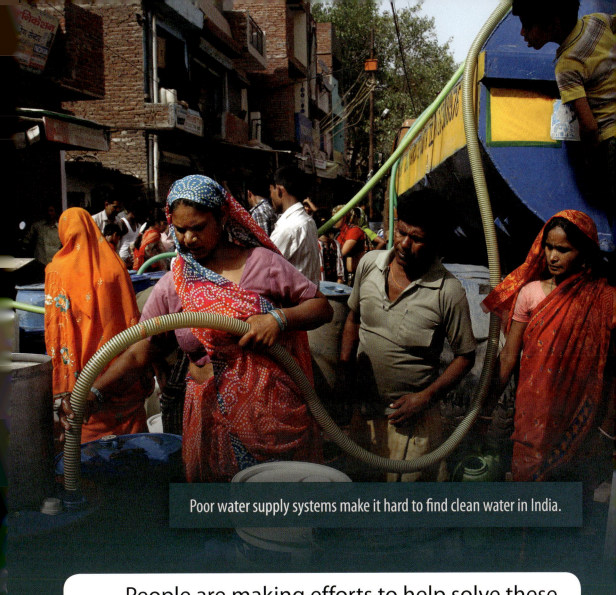

Poor water supply systems make it hard to find clean water in India.

People are making efforts to help solve these problems. To improve water quality, protect the **environment**, and save people's lives, groups such as the World Health Organization (WHO) work to educate people about water safety and improve water access.

CHAPTER NINE

THE PLASTIC PROBLEM

People often use plastic bottles to get water to communities suffering from water scarcity. But plastic is also responsible for many water-related problems.

Ten percent of the trash we create comes from plastic. Landfills, which are areas where trash is buried in the earth, are full of plastic. Plastic doesn't biodegrade, or break down all the way. Chemicals from large pieces of plastic can seep into the soil and groundwater (water that's found underground). These chemicals make their way into rivers and streams over time.

Tiny pieces of plastic called microplastic can be even more harmful. Some are so small that they can't be seen. Fish and birds eat microplastics, which passes them into the food chain.

When plastic waste winds up in the water, animals often mistake it for food.

21

CHAPTER TEN

OCEAN PLASTIC

Plastics can now be found everywhere on the planet—the oceans, the air, even in our bodies! People have found plastics in animals and in the food we eat. Scientists say humans eat about 0.18 ounce (5 g) of plastic each week. That's enough plastic to make a credit card.

There are other plastic problems, too. The Great Pacific Garbage Patch is a huge area of floating plastic in the Pacific Ocean between Hawaii and California. There are about 1.15 million to 2.41 million tons (1 million to 2.2 million mt) of plastic in it.

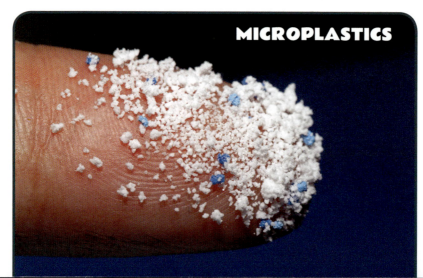

MICROPLASTICS

In October 2019, the Ocean Cleanup's floating barrier collected plastic from the ocean for the first time.

There are many projects to clean up this mess and other plastic problems around the world. As a teen, Dutch inventor Boyan Slat was upset by how much trash he saw in the ocean. He created the Ocean Cleanup. This project uses new technology to catch ocean and river plastics with floating **barriers** and anchored filters.

CHAPTER ELEVEN
WATER RIGHTS

Water can be a political issue. During the 1800s, many Native Americans were moved onto reservations, or areas of land set aside by the government for them to live on. In 1908, the U.S. Supreme Court ruled that Native Americans have special water rights on reservation lands. Still, the government has sometimes ignored that ruling and others. There are still legal battles.

The Dakota Access Pipeline carries oil through part of the United States. Native Americans from the Standing Rock reservation sued the government over the pipeline's construction in 2016 and 2017. They argued that it was harmful to the reservation's land and water. Thousands of Native American water protectors set up camps to try to block the building of the pipeline. However, the pipeline started working in June 2017.

Members of the Sioux Nation and supporters spoke out against the building of the Dakota Access Pipeline.

CHAPTER TWELVE

THE WATER WARRIOR

Autumn Peltier is a member of the Wikwemikong First Nation in Canada. When she was just 8 years old, she started to speak out about water issues, becoming a voice for her community. Since then, she has become a leader in the fight for clean water and is often called a "water warrior."

When Autumn was 12, she spoke to Canadian Prime Minister Justin Trudeau. She told him she didn't agree with Canadian plans that allowed oil pipelines to put waterways at risk. At age 14, she became the chief water commissioner, or person in charge of water, of the Anishinabek Nation.

On World Water Day in 2018, Autumn spoke at the United Nations. She asked world leaders to "warrior up" and protect water just like they protect people.

In 2019, Autumn Peltier was nominated, or put up as a candidate, for the International Children's Peace Prize. She has been nominated three times.

CHAPTER THIRTEEN

HOW TO SAVE WATER

You may not spend much time worrying about how to get clean water. However, water is a limited **resource**, and it's important not to waste it.

Here are some simple ways you can work to save water:

- **Turning off the tap while brushing your teeth could save 8 gallons (30.3 L) each day.**

- **Taking a shower uses 10 to 25 gallons (37.8 to 94.6 L) of water compared to up to 70 gallons (264.9 L) for a bath.**

- **Keep showers to under five minutes long.**

- **Run your dishwasher and washing machines only when you have a full load of dishes or clothes to clean.**

- **Use a bucket of water and sponges to clean your cars and bicycles, not a running hose.**

> Turn off the tap while brushing your teeth. This can save gallons of water each day.

CHAPTER FOURTEEN

BE A WATER WARRIOR

Water is one of the most important natural resources. All plants, animals, and people on Earth need fresh water. Keeping water clean can be hard. Diseases, toxins, and plastic can contaminate water and make people sick. Still, it's important to take care of water. You can join the fight to help protect Earth's water sources.

Small steps at home can make a big difference. Use less water each day. Try to limit the amount of plastic you buy and use. Glass water bottles and cloth grocery bags are great ways to use less plastic. Teach people what you know about water scarcity and how saving water and stopping pollution can help people in need. The choices you make today can help create a better future for our world.

GLOSSARY

activist (AK-tih-vist) Someone who acts strongly in support of or against an issue.

barrier (BAIR-ee-uhr) Something that blocks something from passing.

charcoal (CHAR-kohl) A dark black porous carbon made from vegetable or animal substances.

contaminated (kuhn-TAA-muh-nay-tuhd) Made dangerous, dirty, or impure by having something harmful added to it.

corrosive (kuh-ROH-siv) Capable of wearing away or destroying over time.

environment (ihn-VIY-ruhn-muhnt) The natural world around us.

famine (FA-muhn) A shortage of food that causes people to go hungry.

filter (FIL-tuhr) To pass through something to remove unwanted material, or the thing something is passed through.

membrane (MEM-brayn) A soft, thin layer of living matter that comes from a plant or an animal.

microorganism (my-kroh-OHR-guh-nih-zuhm) A very tiny living thing.

permanent (PUHR-muh-nent) Lasting for a very long time or forever.

pesticide (PEH-stuh-syd) A poison used to kill pests.

resource (REE-sohrs) A usable supply of something.

technology (tek-NAH-luh-jee) A method that uses science to solve problems and the tools used to solve those problems.

INDEX

A
Africa, 16, 17
Agre, Peter, 12, 13

C
Canada, 26
Copeny, Amariyanna, 14

D
Dakota Access Pipeline, 24
dehydration, 18
desalination, 12, 13
diseases, 6, 11, 18, 30
droughts, 4, 16, 18

F
famine, 18
Flint, Michigan, 14

G
germ theory, 11

Gibb, John, 11
Great Pacific Garbage Patch, 22
Gulf of Mexico, 14

I
India, 19

L
lead, 14

M
microorganisms, 7, 11
microplastics, 20, 22

O
Ocean Cleanup, 23

P
Peltier, Autumn, 26
pesticides, 7
plastic, 20, 22, 23, 30

S
Sioux Nation, 24
Slat, Boyan, 23
Standing Rock, 24
Supreme Court, U.S., 24

U
United Nations, 26
United States, 12, 24

W
water scarcity, 16, 17, 18, 20, 30
wells, 6, 7
Wikwemikong First Nation, 26
World Health Organization (WHO), 19

Z
Zimbabwe, 18

PRIMARY SOURCE LIST

Page 11
Harbor in New Jersey. Photograph. January 1, 1890. Corbis via Getty Images.

Page 25
Activists participate in Dakota Access Pipeline protest. Photograph. Jim Watson. December 4, 2016. AFP via Getty Images.

Page 27
Chief Water Commissioner Autumn Peltier addresses the Global Landscapes Forum. Photograph. AP Photo/Richard Drew. Saturday, Sept. 28, 2019. AP Images.

WEBSITES

Due to the changing nature of Internet links, PowerKids Press has developed an online list of websites related to the subject of this book. This site is updated regularly. Please use this link to access the list: www.powerkidslinks.com/SOOF/cleanwater